A BOY
IS SOMETHING SPECIAL

Edited by James L. Murat

Illustrated by Allan Thomas

THE MAKEPEACE COLONY PRESS

A DIVISION OF THE MAKEPEACE COLONY, INC.

STEVENS POINT, WISCONSIN

Third Printing, 1970
Copyright © 1967
By The Makepeace Colony, Incorporated
Printed in the United States of America
SBN 87741-001-1

ACKNOWLEDGMENTS

The editors of THE MAKEPEACE COLONY PRESS deeply appreciate the kind and generous cooperation and interest of the authors and publishers whose permission to include the poetry and prose selected for our little anthologies has made it possible for us to publish this treasury of the worthwhile in remembrance literature.

We have spared no effort to ascertain the ownership of all copyrighted material as well as the authorship of all material, and to secure permission and make full acknowledgment for such use. If we have unintentionally and inadvertently erred in any respect, we express our sincere regrets and will gladly make any necessary corrections and additions in future printings.

Thanks are due to all authors and publishers whose works are included, among whom are the following:

EVERYBODY SAYS reprinted by permission of G. P. Putnam's Sons, publishers, from *All Together* by Dorothy Aldis, copyright 1925-28, 1934, 1939, 1952, by Dorothy Aldis . . . WHAT IS A BOY by Alan Beck, copyright 1950 by New England Mutual Life Insurance Company, Boston, reprinted by permission . . . THE HOUSEWIFE by Catherine Cate Coblentz, reprinted from *The Treasure Chest*, ed. by Charles L. Wallis, by permission of Harper & Row, publishers . . . JUST A BOY reprinted by permission from the book *Best From the Farmers' Almanac*, ed. by Ray Geiger and published by Doubleday and Company . . . PETITION by Angelo Patri and TWO PRAYERS by Andrew Gillies from *The*

A BOY IS SOMETHING SPECIAL

Treasure Chest, ed. by Charles L. Wallis, by permission of Harper & Row, publishers . . . JUST A BOY reprinted by permission from *The Rotarian Magazine* . . . A MOTHER'S BEATITUDE, by Lenora Zearfoss, FOR AN OPEN MIND and THAT LAD OF MINE, authors unknown, and TRUTH by Suzanne Douglass reprinted by permission from *Best From the Farmers' Almanac,* ed. by Ray Geiger and published by Doubleday and Company . . . BUILDING MEN by Robert W. Murphy reprinted by permission from THINK magazine, published by IBM, copyright 1959 by International Business Machines Corporation . . . A BOY TO TRAIN, THE BOY'S IDEAL and EQUIPMENT, all by Edgar A. Guest, reprinted by permission from Henry Regnery Company and Reilly and Lee Company, publishers . . . EVERY CHILD by Edna Casler Joll reprinted by permission of Kenneth Joll and The Curtis Publishing Company . . . ON CHILDREN reprinted from *The Prophet* by Kahlil Gibran with permission of the publisher, Alfred A. Knopf, Inc. copyright 1923 by Kahlil Gibran; renewal copyright 1951 by Administrators C. T. A. of Kahlil Gibran Estate and Mary G. Gibran . . . A SOLDIER'S PRAYER by General Douglas MacArthur reprinted by permission from the May 1965 issue of *The Readers Digest* . . . A MOTHER'S PRAYER by Ruth Simrall Mackoy and PARENT'S PRAYER by Barbara Barnes Orteig reprinted with permission from *Best From the Farmers' Almanac,* ed. by Ray Geiger and published by Doubleday and Company, book copyright 1963 by Almanac Publishing Company . . . BLESSING ON LITTLE BOYS from the book *Death and General Putnam and 101 Other Poems* by Arthur Guiterman, copyright, 1935, by E. P. Dutton & Co., Inc., renewal of copyright in 1963 by Mrs. Vida Lindo Guiterman, reprinted by permission of publishers . . . IF YOU HAVE A LITTLE BOY by Oma Carlyle Anderson, and FOR AN OPEN MIND by Vera White reprinted from *American Album of Poetry,* ed. by Ted Malone, reprinted by permission of Ted Malone Productions.

TO ROSE

"You've shown me where both love and faith abide . . .

You've schooled my mind to reach the ebbing tide,

   To kiss the moon and walk thru early dew;

And tho the sharpest thorns may pierce my flesh,

I still shall pluck the rose because of you."

                                      LESTER

IF YOU HAVE A LITTLE BOY

If you have a little boy
 All your very own,
Then you have enough and more
 To make a happy home.

And if but once each day
 You should see him smile,
That would be enough and more,
 To make your life worth while.

Or, say you have a little boy
  To read to every night,
That would be enough and more
  To make your evenings bright.

And if each night at bed time
  You can kiss this little lad,
That will be enough and more
  To make you very glad.

And if you see him in the evening
  When he kneels to pray,
That will be enough and more
  To make a perfect day.

OMA CARLYLE ANDERSON

EVERYBODY SAYS

Everybody says
I look just like my mother.
Everybody says
I'm the image of Aunt Bee.
Everybody says
My nose is like my father's,
But I want to look like me.

DOROTHY ALDIS

WHAT IS A BOY

BETWEEN THE INNOCENCE of babyhood and the dignity of manhood we find a delightful creature called a boy.

Boys come in assorted sizes, weights, and colors, but all boys have the same creed: To enjoy every second of every minute of every hour of every day and to protest with noise (their only weapon) when their last minute is finished and the adult males pack them off to bed at night.

Boys are found everywhere—on top of, underneath, inside of, climbing on, swinging from, running around, or jumping to. Mothers love them, little girls hate them, older sisters and brothers tolerate them, adults ignore them, and Heaven protects them.

A BOY IS TRUTH with dirt on its face, Beauty with a cut on its finger, Wisdom with bubble gum in its hair, and the Hope of the future with a frog in its pocket.

When you are busy, a boy is an inconsiderate, bothersome, intruding jangle of

noise. When you want him to make a good impression, his brain turns to jelly or else he becomes a savage, sadistic, jungle creature bent on destroying the world and himself with it.

A BOY IS A COMPOSITE—he has the appetite of a horse, the digestion of a sword swallower, the energy of a pocket-size atomic bomb, curiosity of a cat, lungs of a dictator, the imagination of a Paul Bunyan, the shyness of a violet, the audacity of a steel trap, the enthusiasm of a firecracker, and when he makes something, he has five thumbs on each hand.

He likes ice-cream, knives, saws, Christmas, comic books, the boy across the street, woods, water (in its natural habitat), large animals, Dad, trains, Saturday mornings, and fire engines.

He is not much for Sunday School, company, schools, books without pictures, music lessons, neckties, barbers, girls, overcoats, adults, or bedtime.

Nobody else is so early to rise, or so late to supper. Nobody else gets so much fun out of trees, dogs, and breezes. Nobody else can cram into one pocket a rusty knife, a half-eaten apple, three feet of string, an empty Bull Durham sack, two gum drops, six cents, a sling shot, a chunk of unknown substance, and a genuine super-sonic code ring with a secret compartment.

A Boy is a Magical Creature—you can lock him out of your workshop, but you can't lock him out of your heart. You can get him out of your study, but you can't get him out of your mind. Might as well give up—he is your captor, your jailor, your boss, and your master—a freckle-faced, pint-sized, cat-chasing bundle of noise.

But when you come home at night with only the shattered pieces of your hopes and dreams, he can mend them like new with the two magic words—"Hi, Dad!"

ALAN BECK
New England Mutual Life Insurance Co.

Let parents bequeath to their children not riches, but the spirit of reverence.

PLATO

I HAVE A BOY

I've a wonderful boy, and I say to him, "Son,
Be fair and be square in the race you must run.
Be brave if you lose and be meek if you win.
Be better and nobler than I've ever been.
Be honest and noble in all that you do,
And honor the name I have given to you."

I have a boy and I want him to know
We reap in life just about as we sow,
And we get what we earn, be it little or great,
Regardless of luck and regardless of fate.
I will teach him and show him the best that I can,
That it pays to be honest and upright, a man.

I will make him a pal and a partner of mine,
And show him the things in this world that are fine.
I will show him the things that are wicked and bad,
For I figure this knowledge should come from his dad.
I will walk with him, talk with him, play with him, too;

And to all of my promises strive to be true.

We will grow up together, I'll too be a boy,
And share in his trouble and share in his joy.
We'll work out our problems together and then
We will lay out our plans when we both will be men.
And oh, what a wonderful joy this will be,
No pleasure in life could be greater to me.

HUGH M. PIERCE

THE HOUSEWIFE

Jesus, teach me how to be
Proud of my simplicity.

Sweep the floors, wash the clothes,
Gather for each vase a rose.

Iron and tend a tiny frock,
Keeping one eye on the clock.

Always having time kept free
For childish questions asked of me.

Grant me wisdom Mary had
When she taught her little Lad.

CATHERINE CATE COBLENTZ

JUST A BOY

Got to understand the lad—
He's not eager to be bad;
If the right he always knew,
He would be as old as you.

Were he now exceeding wise,
He'd be just about your size;
When he does things that annoy,
Don't forget—he's just a boy.

Could he know and understand,
He would need no guiding hand;
But he's young and hasn't learned
How life's corners must be turned.

Doesn't know from day to day
There is more in life than play,
More to face than selfish joy,
Don't forget—he's just a boy.

Being just a boy he'll do
Much you will not want him to;
He'll be careless of his ways,
Have his disobedient days.

Wilful, wild and headstrong, too,
He'll sometimes make his parents blue.
Things of value he'll destroy,
But reflect—he's just a boy.

Just a boy who needs a friend,
Patient, kindly to the end;
Needs a father who will show
Him the things he wants to know.

Take him with you when you walk,
Listen when he wants to talk,
His companionship enjoy.
Don't forget—he's just a boy.

                            ANONYMOUS

PETITION

I Have a Boy to Bring Up. Help me to perform my task with wisdom, kindness, and good cheer. Help me always to see him clearly, as he is. Let not my pride hide his faults. Let not my fear for him magnify my doubts and fears until I make him doubting and fearful in his turn. Quicken my judgment so that I shall know how to train him to think as a child, to be in all things pure and simple as a child.

I Have a Boy to Bring Up. Give me great patience and a long memory. Let me remember the hard places of my own youth, so that I may help when I see him struggling as I struggled then. Let me remember the things that made me glad, lest I, sweating in the toil and strain of life, forget that a child's laughter is the light of life.

I Have a Boy to Bring Up. Teach me that love understandeth all things, knows no weakness, tolerates no selfishness. Keep me from weakening my son through granting him pleasures that end in pain, ease of body that brings sickness of soul, and a vision of life that ends in death. Grant that I may love my son wisely and myself not at all.

I HAVE A SON TO BRING UP. Give him the values and beauty and just rewards of industry. Give him an understanding brain and hands that are cunning that he may work out his own happiness.

I HAVE A BOY TO BRING UP. Help me to send him into the world with a mission of service. Strengthen my mind and heart that I may teach him that he is his brother's keeper. Grant that he may serve those who know not the need of service, and not knowing, need it the most.

I HAVE A BOY TO BRING UP. So guide and direct me that I may do this service to the glory of God, the service of my country, and to my son's happiness.

ANGELO PATRI

Blessed be the hand that prepares a pleasure for a child, for there is no saying when and where it may bloom forth.

JERROLD

THE LITTLE CHAP WHO FOLLOWS ME

A careful man I ought to be;
A little fellow follows me;
I do not dare to go astray
For fear he'll go the self-same way.

I must not madly step aside,
Where pleasure's paths are smooth and wide,
And join in wine's red revelry—
A little fellow follows me.

I cannot once escape his eyes;
Whate'er he sees me do he tries—
Like me, he says, he's going to be;
The little chap who follows me.

He thinks that I am good and fine,
Believes in every word of mine;
The base in me he must not see,
The little chap who follows me.

I must remember as I go,
Through summer's sun and winter's snow,
I'm building for the years to be,
A little fellow follows me.

AUTHOR UNKNOWN

WILLOW WHISTLE

Only a boy
Can set free
The music in
A willow tree.

Can find the cricket
And the lark
Hidden in
A willow's bark.

Can fife and flute,
Can lilt and croon
The notes that make
A willow tune.

Can blow an air
Winged as a thistle
From a little
Willow whistle.

ETHEL ROMIG FULLER

From WE THANK THEE

For mother-love and father-care,
For brothers strong and sisters fair,
For love at home and here each day,
For guidance lest we go astray,
    Father in Heaven, we thank Thee.

UNKNOWN

If a child lives with criticism, he learns to condemn.

If a child lives with hostility, he learns to fight.

If a child lives with fear, he learns to be apprehensive.

If a child lives with pity, he learns to feel sorry for himself.

If a child lives with ridicule, he learns to be shy.

If a child lives with jealousy, he learns to be envious.

If a child lives with shame, he learns to feel guilty.

If a child lives with encouragement, he learns to be confident.

If a child lives with tolerance, he learns to be patient.

If a child lives with praise, he learns to be appreciative.

If a child lives with acceptance, he learns to love.

If a child lives with approval, he learns to like himself.

If a child lives with recognition, he learns that it is good to have a goal.

If a child lives with honesty and fairness, he learns what truth and justice are.

If a child lives with security, he learns to have faith in himself and those about him.

If a child lives with friendliness, he learns that the world is a nice place in which to live.

If YOU live in serenity, your child will live with peace of mind.

AUTHOR UNKNOWN

TWO PRAYERS

Last night my little boy confessed to me
Some childish wrong;
And kneeling at my knee,
He prayed with tears—
"Dear God, make me a man
Like Daddy — wise and strong;
I know you can."

Then while he slept
I knelt beside his bed,
Confessed my sins,
And prayed with low-bowed head—
"O God, make me a child
Like my child here—
Pure, guileless,
Trusting Thee with the faith sincere."

ANDREW GILLIES

JUST A BOY

AFTER A MALE BABY has grown out of long clothes, and triangles, and has acquired pants, and freckles, and so much dirt that relatives do not dare to kiss it between meals, it becomes a BOY.

A boy can swim like a fish, run like a deer, climb like a squirrel, balk like a mule, bellow like a bull, eat like a pig, or act like a jackass, according to climatic conditions.

He is a piece of skin stretched over an appetite. A noise, covered with smudges.

HE IS CALLED A TORNADO because he comes at the most unexpected times, hits the most unexpected places, and leaves everything a wreck behind him.

He is a growing animal of superlative promise, to be fed and watered and kept warm.

He is a joy forever, a periodic nuisance, the problem of our times, and hope of a nation. Every boy is evidence that God is not discouraged by man.

Were it not for boys, the newspapers would go unread, and a thousand picture shows would go bankrupt.

BOYS ARE USEFUL in running errands. A boy can easily do the family errands with the aid of five or six adults. The zest with which a boy does an errand is equaled only by the speed of a turtle on a July day.

The boy is a natural spectator. He watches parades, fires, fights, ball games, automobiles, boats, and airplanes with equal fervor, but not the clock.

Boys faithfully imitate their dads in spite of all efforts to teach them good manners.

A boy, if not washed too often and if kept in a cool, quiet place after each accident, will survive broken bones, hornets, swimming holes, fights, and nine helpings of pie.

THE ROTARIAN

A child is not a vessel to be filled, but a lamp to be lighted.

A MOTHER'S BEATITUDE

Blessed is the mother who understands her child, for she shall inherit a kingdom of memories.

Blessed is the mother who knows how to comfort, for she shall possess a child's devotion.

Blessed is the mother who guides by the path of righteousness, for she shall be proud of her offspring.

Blessed is the mother who teaches respect, for she shall be respected.

Blessed is the mother who emphasizes the good and minimizes the bad, for in like manner the child shall make evaluations.

Blessed is the mother who treats her child as she would be treated, for her home shall be filled with happiness.

Blessed is the mother who answers simply the startling questions, for she shall always be trusted.

Blessed is the mother who has character strong enough to withstand the thoughtless remarks and resentments of the growing child, for again, in due time, she shall be honored.

LENORA ZEARFOSS

TWO IN BED

When my brother Tommy
Sleeps in bed with me,
He doubles up
And makes
himself
exactly
like

a

V

and 'cause the bed is not so wide,
A part of him is on my side.

A. B. ROSS

BUILDING MEN

How do you train him?
There he stands before you,
Clean and lanky,
With a look of bright morning on his face.
Appealing
In the way that morning is,
And youth is,
And the hopefulness of youth.

And then you realize
  The awful responsibility
  That is yours
To train.
To train and build,
And nurture and lead.
You realize how much of business is training,
How much of modern industry is building men,
  Inspiring men,
And leading them to achievement.

Well, here is good timber
But what are you going to build of it?
And how do you go about the building process?
This is the answer:
You give him of yourself.
Urge him to learn his craft of course,
And learn it well,

Whatever it is—law, accounting, engineering.
Tell him he must labor hard, to learn it well.
Then, of course,
Goad him to dip into classic tomes
And newer letters
To touch base often
In academic halls
And move about in tasks foreign and unfamiliar.
But this young man needs more.
Judgment he needs,
And understanding,
And maturity.

For these, he looks to you
And you must give them to him.

Let yourself rub off on him,
Let him sit beside you as you work,
To work with you,
To study with you,
To be perplexed with you,
To analyze with you,
And to dream with you.

Give him the impossible task to do,
   The unanswerable question to answer.
There is no better way to train—
Whether you be Socrates training Athenian youth,

Or an American man of business
Teaching some young hopeful the craft
    of management
In mid-century industrial America.

> ROBERT W. MURPHY
> *from THINK Magazine,*
> by International Business
> Machines Corporation

A BOY TO TRAIN

The man who has a boy to train,
    Has work to keep him night and day.
There's much to him he must explain,
    And many a doubt to clear away;
His task is one which calls for tact
    And friendship of the finest kind,
Because, with every word and act,
    He molds the little fellow's mind.
He must be careful of his speech,
    For careless words are quickly learned;
He must be wise enough to teach
    What corners may be safely turned.

> EDGAR A. GUEST

OUR BABY HAS RED HAIR

Our baby has red hair
But we don't care.
  He has eyes as blue
  As his daddy's too.
And we don't care
If he *has* red hair.

Our baby has red hair,
But we don't care.
  He has a gurgly coo,
  And he chuckles, too.
And we don't care
If he *has* red hair.

Our baby has red hair,
But we don't care,
  He'll laugh and play
  With us all day.
And we don't care;
We *like* red hair.

PETRUCCHIO'S KATE
Chicago Tribune

Children's children are the crown of old men; and the glory of children are their fathers.

PROVERBS 17:6

EVERY CHILD

Every child should know a hill,
And the clean joy of running down its
   long slope
With the wind in his hair.
He should know a tree—
The comfort of its cool lap of shade,
And the supple strength of its arms
Balancing him between earth and sky
So he is the creature of both.
He should know bits of singing water—
The strange mysteries in its depths,
And the long sweet grasses that border it.
Every child should know some scrap
Of uninterrupted sky, to shout against;
And have one star, dependable and
   bright,
For wishing on.

                                EDNA CASLER JOLL

ON CHILDREN

... Your children are not your children.
They are the sons and daughters of Life's longing for itself.
They come through you but not from you,
And though they are with you yet they belong not to you.
You may give them your love but not your thoughts,
For they have their own thoughts.
You may house their bodies but not their souls,
For their souls dwell in the house of tomorrow, which you cannot visit, not even in your dreams.
You may strive to be like them, but seek not to make them like you.
For life goes not backward nor tarries with yesterday . . .

KAHLIL GIBRAN
From The Prophet

FOR AN OPEN MIND

I must grant you, my son, the right to think,
   I must not fill your mind with outworn fears;
You must remain an open soul to drink
   The changing ideas of the changing years.
Great seems my wisdom to you now you're young,
   I must take care lest I too think it so;
Too long, I fear, to ancient forms I've clung,
   You must not heed my credo; you must grow.

The things I work for, how I vote or pray;
   May foolish seem to you, or even wrong.
Well, you are free to seek a better way!
   Your mind is healthy when your doubt is strong.
Too long has age been synonym for truth;
   My son, seek your own answers; you are youth!

VERA WHITE

THAT LAD OF MINE

To feel his little hand in mine, so clinging and so warm,
To know he thinks me strong enough to keep him safe from harm;

To see his simple faith in all that I can say or do,
It sort o' shames a fellow, but it makes him better, too;

And I'm trying hard to be the man he fancies me to be,
Because I have this lad at home who thinks the world o' me.

I would not disappoint his trust for anything on earth,
Nor let him know how little I just naturally am worth.

But after all, it's easier, that brighter road to climb,
With the little hands behind me to push me all the time.

And I reckon I'm a better man than what I used to be
Because I have this lad at home who thinks the world o' me.

AUTHOR UNKNOWN

AT THE SAME TIME came the disciples unto Jesus, saying, Who is the greatest in the kingdom of heaven?

And Jesus called a little child unto him, and set him in the midst of them, and said, Verily I say unto you, Except ye be converted, and become as little children, ye shall not enter into the kingdom of heaven.

WHOSOEVER THEREFORE shall humble himself as this little child, the same is greatest in the kingdom of heaven.

And whoso shall receive one such little child in my name receiveth me.

But whoso shall offend one of these little ones which believe in me, it were better for him that a millstone were hanged about his neck, and that he were drowned in the depth of the sea.

MATT. 18: 1-6

He that believeth and is baptized shall be saved.

MARK 16: 16

THE BOY'S IDEAL

I must be fit for a child to play with,
Fit for a youngster to walk away with;
  Fit for his trust and fit to be
  Ready to take him upon my knee;
Whether I win or I lose my fight,
I must be fit for my boy at night.

I must be fit for a child to come to,
Speech there is that I must be dumb to;
  I must be fit for his eyes to see,
  He must find nothing of shame in me;
Whatever I make of myself, I must
Square to my boy's unfaltering trust.

I must be fit for a child to follow,
Scorning the places where loose men wallow;
  Knowing how much he shall learn from me,
  I must be fair as I'd have him be;
I must come home to him, day by day,
Clean as the morning I went away.

I must be fit for a child's glad greeting,
His are eyes that there is no cheating;
  He must behold me in every test,
  Not at my worst, but my very best;
He must be proud when my life is done
To have men know that he is my son.

EDGAR A. GUEST
All That Matters

Part of the spiritual legacy that General of the Army Douglas MacArthur left to his son, Arthur, was a prayer. The General wrote it during the desperate early days of the Pacific war.

A SOLDIER'S PRAYER FOR HIS SON

BUILD ME A SON, O Lord, who will be strong enough to know when he is weak, brave enough to face himself when he is afraid; one who will be proud and unbending in honest defeat, humble and gentle in victory.

Build me a son whose wishes will not take the place of deeds; a son who will know Thee — and that to know himself is the foundation stone of knowledge.

LEAD HIM, I PRAY, not in the path of ease and comfort, but under the stress and spur of difficulties and challenge. Let him learn to stand up in the storm; let him learn compassion for those who fail.

BUILD ME A SON whose heart will be clear, whose goal will be high; a son who will master himself before he seeks to master other men; one who will reach into the future, yet never forget the past. And after all these things are his, add, I pray, enough of a sense of humor so that he may always be serious yet never take himself too seriously. Give him humility, the simplicity of true greatness, the open mind of true wisdom and the meekness of true strength.

Then I, his father, will dare to whisper, "I have not lived in vain."

GENERAL DOUGLAS MACARTHUR

TEN DO'S AND DON'TS FOR PARENTS

1. Treat all your children with equal affection.
2. Keep close to them.
3. Make their friends welcome in your home.
4. Don't quarrel in front of them.
5. Be thoughtful to each other.
6. Never lie to them.
7. Always answer their questions.
8. Don't punish them in the presence of others.
9. Be constant in your affection and moods.
10. Concentrate on good points, not failings.

CHRISTOPHER NEWS NOTES

EQUIPMENT

Figure it out for yourself, my lad,
You've all that the greatest of men have had,
Two arms, two hands, two legs, two eyes
And brain to use if you would be wise.
With this equipment they all began,
So start for the top and say, "I can."

Look them over, the wise and great,
They take their food from a common plate,
And similar knives and forks they use,
With similar laces they tie their shoes,
The world considers them brave and smart,
But you've all they had when they made their start.

You can triumph and come to skill,
You can be great if you only will.
You're well equipped for what fight you choose,
You have legs and arms and a brain to use,
And the man who has risen great deeds to do
Began his life with no more than you.

You are the handicap you must face,
You are the one who must choose your place,
You must say where you want to go,
How much you will study the truth to know.
God has equipped you for life, but He
Lets you decide what you want to be.

Courage must come from the soul within,
The man must furnish the will to win.
So figure it out for yourself, my lad.
You were born with all that the great have had,
With your equipment they all began —
Get hold of yourself, and say: *"I can."*

EDGAR A. GUEST

TRUTH

His little toy dog is covered with dust
And so are his little toy blocks.
I bought them and paid an extravagant price,
So what does he play with — *the box.*

SUZANNE DOUGLASS

FOR A CHILD

Your friends shall be the Tall Wind,
   The River and the Tree;
The Sun that laughs and marches,
   The Swallows and the Sea.

Your prayers shall be the murmur
   Of grasses in the rain;
The song of wildwood thrushes
   That makes God glad again.

And you shall run and wander,
   And you shall dream and sing
Of brave things and bright things
   Beyond the swallow's wings.

And you shall envy no man,
   Nor hurt your heart with sighs,
For I will keep you simple
   That God may make you wise.

FANNY STEARNS DAVIS

I FOUND GOD

Sophisticated, worldly-wise,
I searched for God and found Him not,
Until one day, the world forgot,
I found Him in my baby's eyes.

MARY AFTON THACKER

Rock-a-bye, baby, thy cradle is green;
Father's a nobleman, mother's a queen;
Betty's a lady, and wears a gold ring;
And Johnny's a drummer, and drums for
    the king.

MOTHER GOOSE RHYME

What are little boys made of?
Snips and snails and puppy dogs' tails,
That's what little boys are made of.

A BOY I KNOW

He's not a witty boy, nor wise,
    He has not much of outward grace;
And yet the sparkle of his eyes,
    The morning sunshine of his face,
Oft make a little glow of cheer,
Whenever he is passing near.

I hear his whistle up the street,
    I hear his merry laugh ring out;
I hear the rush of sturdy feet,
    I hear his free and boyish shout —
And then I smile and straight forget
My newest care, my latest fret.

His hands are rough, but they are strong,
    And never have been known to shirk;
And blithe and cheery is the song
    He hums when at his daily work;
For any task seems well worth while
To him who takes it with a smile.

Those hands are very tender, too,
    And gentle with the maimed and weak,
And oft a kindly service do
    Of which the boy will never speak.
God bless this modest, manly boy,
Who makes all duty but a joy!

And when he reaches man's estate,
  God keep him good and sweet as now,
For then no adverse stroke of fate
  Shall cloud that fair and open brow;
The manly boy can only grow
To manly manhood — this I know!

ANONYMOUS

LULLABYE

Sleep, my child, and peace attend thee,
  All through the night;
Guardian angels God will lend thee,
  All through the night;
Soft the drowsy hours are creeping,
Hill and vale in slumber sleeping,
Mother dear her watch is keeping,
  All through the night.

God is here, thou'lt not be lonely,
  All through the night;
'Tis not I who guards thee only,
  All through the night.
Night's dark shades will soon be over,
Still my watchful care shall hover,
God with me His watch is keeping,
  All through the night.

FROM THE WELSH

A MOTHER'S PRAYER

Make Me a Wise Mother, O Lord. Keep me calm and give me patience to bear the small, irritating things in the daily routine of life.

Give me tolerance and understanding to bridge the gulf between my generation and that of my children.

Let me not be too ready to guide my children's stumbling feet, but allow me to be ever near to bind their bruises.

Give me a sense of humor that I may laugh with them but never at them.

Let Me Refrain from preaching with words. Keep me from forcing their confidences, but give me a sympathetic ear when my children come to me.

Help me to teach them that life must not be filled with compromises, but must be replete with victories.

Make me humble.

Keep my children close to me, O Lord, though miles may separate us.

And let Thy light so shine upon me that they, too, will perceive Thy glory. Amen

RUTH SIMRALL MACKOY

BROTHER'S OPINION
OF THE BABY

Mother's brought a baby,
  Little bit o' thing;
Think that I could put him
  Through my rubber ring.

Ain't he awful ugly?
  Ain't he awful pink?
"Just come down from Heaven,"
  That's a fib, I think.

The doctor told another
  Great big awful lie;
My nose ain't out of joint,
  That's not why I cry.

Think I ought to love him!
  No, I won't! So there!
Naughty crying baby
  Ain't got any hair.

Send me off with Biddy
  Every single day;
"Be a good boy, Charlie,
  Run away and play."

Got all *my* nice kisses,
  Got *my* place in bed;
Mean to take my drumstick
  And beat him on the head.

BLESSING ON LITTLE BOYS

God bless all little boys who look like
   Puck,
With wide eyes, wider mouths and stick-
   out ears,
Rash little boys who stay alive by luck
And Heaven's favor in this world of tears,
Ten-thousand-question-asking little
   boys,
Rapid of hand and foot and thought as
   well,
Playing with gorgeous fancies more than
   toys,
Heroes of what they dream, but never
   tell;
Father, in your vast playground let them
   know
The loveliness of ocean, star, and hill;
Protect from every bitterness and woe
Your heedless little acolytes, and still
Grant me the grace, I beg upon my
   knees,
Not to forget that I was one of these.

ARTHUR GUITERMAN

Boys will be boys.

EDWARD BULWER-LYTTON

PARENT'S PRAYER

Dear God, please make him strong
Of body, mind and soul
Please let him know the right from wrong
The weak thoughts from the whole.

Let we his parents guide his way
To peace and harmony.
Please help us in his work and play
To bring him close to Thee.

Dear Lord, we thank You for this child
You have put in our care.
Please bless his eyes that are so mild,
His hands and feet and hair.

Please keep him safe from all known ill
And grow to be a man
So he may follow out Thy will
On earth, as best he can.

A parent's Prayer we bring to You
Who are so wise and kind.
Dear God, watch all that we may do.
Without Thee we are blind.

            BARBARA ORTEIG

Children need models more than they need critics.

            JOSEPH JOUBERT

The Makepeace Colony is dedicated to the idea of sharing with you the inspiration, joy and comfort that we have found in the selections contained in this series — to bring you "a treasury of the worthwhile in remembrance literature." We hope you have found our little volumes a pleasure to give, and a delight to receive.

If you have written or found selections which you would like to share with others in future editions of this series, we invite you to forward them to us.

This little volume was designed and illustrated by Allan Thomas. The type is 12 Baskerville, the text paper is a 70 lb. white offset stock, vellum finish, and the printing is a combination of letterpress and offset, with hard covers and Smyth sewed binding — all designed to make this series of remembrance gift literature of lasting value.

THE MAKEPEACE COLONY PRESS